MW00898185

The Pirate and the Pri[...]
by D. M. Larson

Copyright © 2015 All Rights Reserved

For permission to perform this play,
contact doug@freedrama.net

SCENE 1

(Half the stage is pirate ship, other half is princess room/balcony of a castle. Bones is a pirate girl who is pacing the ship annoyed)

BONES
I am sick of being at sea. I want to feel solid ground. Oh... To take a nice warm bath... Instead of washing in freezing cold sea water. You see what the sea has done to my hair!

(Removes hat or bandana to reveal a mess)

BONES (CONT.)
No more pirate's life for me. No more yo ho with these yo-yos. I am tired of all the bottles and bums. I want to drink from a chilled glass goblet... And have some ice cold milk. Fresh cool milk... and ice... a glass of ice water would even be nice. And you know what else you get when you mix milk and ice... this incredible thing called ice cream. You'll never find that on a pirate ship. I'd give anything for a scoop. But you'll never find anything like that on this rust bucket... no milk, no ice cream, not even an itty bitty ice cube... How come the most wonderful things spoil so quickly?

(SLY enters)

BONES (CONT.)
And I am tired of you too, Sly. Go away.

SLY
It's not my fault you're stuck on this ship.

BONES
I have to blame someone.

SLY
Anything I can do to help?

BONES
Actually, yes.

(She sticks a bucket on his head or stuffs him in a barrel)

SLY
Feel better?

BONES
A little. That's the pirate way. Take out your
frustrations on others. But that's not nice is it?

SLY
Nice? Since when are pirates nice?

BONES
I am tired of being mean.

SLY
But you're so good at it.

BONES
Har, har.

SLY
I heard a rumor…

BONES
So?

SLY
And it's about you.

BONES
Pirates love to gossip.

SLY
Don't you want to know what they said?

BONES
I know how you are... It's gonna cost me.

SLY
Of course.

BONES
Then I'm not interested.

SLY
You're no fun.

BONES
Don't you have to go swab the deck or something,
cabin boy?

SLY
Fine... I will tell you. Just promise you won't let "you
know who" I gave you something for free.

BONES
Pirate's honor... For whatever that's worth.

SLY
I heard that you're getting promoted from scallywag
to sea dog.

BONES
What? Really? Why?

SLY
I think it is because of that jeweled dagger you stole
from the King of Acapulco.

BONES
I didn't steal it. The king dropped it. And when I tried to return it, he accused me of stealing it, so I ran.

SLY
Well, I know that but the others heard a slightly different tale. Spun by you…

BONES
Great so I am getting promoted based on a lie.

SLY
More of a tall tale based in fact.

BONES
Whatever... It's still not true.

SLY
Pirates tell tall tales all the time. Our own captain of this here ship tells the tallest. He loves that story of fighting with a giant octopus. The part where he ties all the legs on knots is hard to swallow. And the octopus gets bigger every time he tells the tale.

BONES
Fine. You made your point

(She starts to go)

SLY
Where you going?

BONES
To do a little spying

(He is alone)

SLY
She is something isn't she? But she hardly notices me. I just annoy her. I try to be extra nice to her... Remember that golden tooth I gave her? The one I stole from Old Stinky when he was sleeping?

SLY (CONT.)
She didn't even wear it. She'd look so good with a
golden tooth. And then there is that sea slug I
caught her for a pet. I never see her with it. I just
wish I knew what would make her happy. Nothing
on this ship, that's for sure, especially not me.

(He exits sadly. Old Stinky enters... Bones sneaks around in a disguise -
inside a barrel maybe)

STINKY
Back here again... The place where I started from.
Dare I call it home? Home for me has been this
ship for so long. But lately it has felt like something
has been missing. And I finally know what. It's the
woman I left behind. No adventure or treasure has
been enough to fill void she left. I must win her
back. I must let her know much she means to me. I
need to give Bones something really tough to do.
Something that will take her a long time so I am can
put my plan in motion. There are a lot of old
wounds I must heal and it will not be fixed quickly
or easily. But I can't go on without her anymore.

(Stinky notices Bones)

STINKY
Come on out, Bones. You could fool a landlubber,
but not an old fooler like me.

BONES
So what's this I hear about a promotion?

STINKY
Aw... Your spying skills are better than I thought...
Yes, Bones. The Captain and me think ye ready.
We have a job for you. We want you to row
ashore…

BONES
To land? Really? Solid ground…

STINKY
Been awhile eh?

BONES
Too long.

STINKY
Then you'll like this.

BONES
Definitely. Anything to get me off this garbage scow
and on to something that doesn't shake and move
and toss and turn. Solid ground. How do I love
thee?

STINKY
We want you to steal the pink diamond of Princess
Fuchsia.

BONES
Princess Fushia? But that castle is impossible to
get in to.

STINKY
Not for a clever sneak like you. It might take awhile.
Take all the time ye need.

BONES
Really? I can take my time?

STINKY
Just don't come back without the diamond... Take a
row boat and one crew member... Keep it small so
they don't notice you.

BONES
I'll take Sly.

STINKY
I don't know. That boy is a bit too goofy around ye.

BONES
I'll whip him into shape.

STINKY
All right then. We approach the castle waters at midnight. Be ready to row ashore.

BONES
Ay ay sir.

STINKY
I ain't no sir. Save your salutes for someone who cares. Make us proud girl.

(STINKY exits)

BONES
This is it. This is my chance to get off the stinky old rust bucket. Take as long as I need. Well I need a long time. A really long time... First thing I'll find is a cow to get myself some fresh milk. Then I'll buy a pretty gown all made of comfy silk. And I'll take a warm bath for nearly half a day. Then find a feather bed to sleep the night away. And the next day too. "Land ho! Land ho! That's where I want to go. Land ho! Land ho! I will set the world aglow."

(Sly enters)

SLY
I heard you need a crew member for a special secret mission.

BONES
That's right. You up for the challenge?

SLY
I was born ready.

BONES
I need to borrow some treasure from some of the others. I have numerous expenses coming up.

SLY
Borrow?

BONES
Just like they borrowed from the ships we
plundered. Perhaps we can find the owners of the
treasure when we get to land and give it back..

SLY
Yeah right. Like that will happen.

(They exit)

END OF SCENE

SCENE 2

(Princess Fuchsia is on the balcony looking out at the audience which is the sea. Nanny approaches her)

NANNY
Come inside. You'll catch your death of cold.

FUCHSIA
I can't get enough of the sea. I love the smell and the way the sun dances on the waters. Can't I go down to the beach?

NANNY
Them waters is dangerous miss. And you don't even know how to swim.

FUCHSIA
I just want to dip my foot in the water... feel it... I don't even know what it feels like! Stuck in this castle all the time. It drives me mad.

NANNY
But you're safe. There's so many dangers out there. It's not safe for any girl, especially not a princess.

FUCHSIA
What good is all this if I can't even enjoy life?

NANNY
You have way more than any other girl can dream of. You're spoiled.

FUCHSIA
You don't understand at all.

NANNY
I understand more than you know. I've been out there missy and it's not all it's cracked up to be. I've lost a lot being out there including my heart.

FUCHSIA
What? There's someone you love out there?

NANNY
But he broke my heart. He romanced me. Bought
me gifts. Took me to the finest restaurants. Spoiled
me rotten... then I found out where he got his
fortunes... he was a pirate.

(Fuchsia is more excited than scared)

FUCHSIA
Oh my goonie gracious. A real pirate?!

NANNY
He stole my heart like he stole his treasures but
broke it in the end. See... I couldn't love a pirate.

FUCHSIA
Why not?

NANNY
Why not?! Are you mad? That's no life for a woman
of virtue.

FUCHSIA
Is it dangerous?

(FUCHSIA is excited at the idea)

NANNY
Very.

FUCHSIA
With lots of peril?

NANNY
That's the same thing, dear.

FUCHSIA
Never boring or dull?

NANNY

Now you stop with that talk. You should be scared
of all that. Boring and dull suits me just fine. Better
safe than sorry. Come back inside now. It's getting
dark.

(Nanny goes inside but Fuchsia stays. Bones and Sly sneak up during
the following and listen)

FUCHSIA

I'm not going inside until I see the sunset. The
sunset is the most beautiful part of my day. Sure,
daddy buys me whatever I want. I have all the
lovely dresses and jewelry a girl could ever wish for
but there's something about a sunset, so magical
and unexpected... it's never the same. I treasure
that magical moment when the sun touches the sea
and sets it on fire. To touch the sea... How I long to
feel the ocean waves... To be free to sail your
waters... I would give anything to leave this tower
and see where the sun sleeps on the edge of the
world. It must be an amazing place... More magical
than any place on earth. A warm and loving place.
Somewhere I can be free.

(Fucshia goes inside and Bones and Sly come closer)

BONES

This is too easy. There's no guards or anything.

SLY

Easy? We spent two days exploring the town and
two more days hiking and scouting around the cliffs
surrounding the castle. And then it took an entire
day to climb the cliffs to get to this spot.

(SLY looks and gets dizzy)

SLY (CONT.)
Don't look down, don't look down.

BONES
I told you that you could stay with the boat.

SLY
But it's fun hanging out with you.

BONES
You have a funny way of showing it; complaining
the whole time.

SLY
I just don't understand why it took so long to get to
this point.

BONES
I'm very careful, okay? And maybe I've enjoyed
being on land for a change.

SLY
So that's what this is all about. You turned this into
a little vacation for yourself.

BONES
Old Stinky said to take my time.

SLY
That's odd. I wonder why?

BONES
No clue. Seemed weird but I'm not complaining.

SLY
So you gonna go get the princess's pink jewel?

BONES
She doesn't sound like she cares much for jewels.
Maybe we can make some kind of trade.

SLY
Trade?

BONES

What's something piratey we can give her? She
seems excited about pirates. Maybe she'd like
something of ours in trade for her jewel?

SLY

How about some smelly pirate socks?

BONES

Maybe she'd like my hat or something. Let's go ask
her.

SLY

You're just going to waltz in there and talk to her?

BONES

Sure, why not?

SLY

And if she screams and alerts the guards?

BONES

We throw her into the sea.

SLY

Nice.

BONES

Here she comes. Stay hidden. Seeing two of so
might scare her.

FUCHSIA

Good night, nanny. Sleep well. Yes, I'm in bed. No,
I won't go outside again tonight.

(Fucshia comes out)

FUCHSIA (CONT.)
Evening star, wishing star, first star of night
I will share my wish with you tonight
I wish for adventure and a journey by sea
I wish to spread my wings and to be free
Make me someone new and transform me
Give me this secret wish, a pirate's life at sea

(Bones comes out of hiding)

BONES
Perhaps I can make your wish come true.

FUCHSIA
Who... who are you?

BONES
I'm your fairy godmother.

FUCHSIA
Really? You don't look like a fairy godmother... you
look more like…

(Fuchsia gasps)

BONES
A pirate.

FUCHSIA
A real pirate?

BONES
Ay! I be a pirate.

FUCHSIA
I've never seen a real pirate before. There are girl
pirates too?

BONES
A few.

FUCHSIA

This is amazing. I've always wanted to meet a real
pirate. Can you stay awhile and talk? I want to
hear all about pirates and your adventures.

BONES

Well, uh... I guess I can stay... so you're not afraid?

FUCHSIA

Should I be?

BONES

Depends... I'm hear to make a trade. I need
something you've got and I'd be happy to trade my
time and some pirate tales and even my hat for
something of yours.

FUCHSIA

What is it you seek?

BONES

A rare pink jewel. About this big.

FUCHSIA

Oh, that one. It's so gaudy. I hate it.

BONES

So you'll give it to me?

FUCHSIA

For a trade...

BONES

No problem... here's my hat and get ready for some
amazing tales from the sea.

FUCHSIA

No, we trade for something else. I want us to trade
places.

BONES

Huh?

FUCHSIA
We look a little bit alike. Same age. Similar height. I
can do you all up in a wig and makeup and such.
I'm always dressing up and playing pretend. They
hardly ever let me out of my room so it's just my
nanny you need to fool really. And I can wear your
stuff and mess myself up a bit... get some dirt on
my face... finally some dirt on my face!

BONES
So I could stay here... in your room... free hot
meals…

FUCHSIA
All you can eat.

BONES
Warm baths?

FUCHSIA
As warm as you like.

BONES
And comfy pillows?

FUCHSIA
It will be like sleeping on clouds.

BONES
You really want to be a pirate?

FUCHSIA
I've dreamed about it since forever. This would be a
dream come true.

BONES
It's not easy.

FUCHSIA
I'm tired of easy.

BONES
You'll get so dirty you'll forget what it's like to be
clean.

FUCHSIA
I hate taking baths.

BONES
This just might work.

(SLY comes out of hiding)

FUCHSIA
Oh! My! Another pirate! And a boy!

SLY
Sorry if I scared you miss, but I had to put a stop to
this.

BONES
Sly, please. I need a break. I'm drowning out there.
I need some solid ground. I need to relax. I need to
be pampered. I know it seems like I'm rough and
tough but I am still a girl under all this dirt. Besides,
she won't turn over the jewel we need unless we do
the switch.

SLY
What if we just take it from her?

(Sly suddenly moves toward the Princess who shrieks and then the Princess grabs
something and hits him over the head. He falls to the floor)

BONES
You okay, Sly?

SLY
She packs a wallop.

FUCHSIA
I have training in hand to hand combat. Father
doesn't believe in a princess being helpless. I can
hold my own in a fight.

SLY
I think she hits harder than you, Bones.

BONES
Oh, yeah?

(Bones punches him)

SLY
Okay, maybe not.

BONES
This is Sly…

SLY
Her friend.

BONES
My associate.

SLY
Brother in arms.

BONES
Guilty by association.

FUCHSIA
I've never been around pirates before. I thought
they'd be scarier.

BONES
He's had a bath recently. He gets way scarier.

SLY
Funny.

BONES
I thought so.

FUCHSIA
So how do I become a pirate?

SLY
You're really going through with this?

(Bones looks at Fuchsia who nods then Sly who scowls at her. Then back again. Fuchsia pulls out some perfume and sprays it. Bones smells it and gives a big smile)

BONES
I am!

FUCHSIA
Huzzah!

SLY
This is crazy.

BONES
Now we need to teach you to be a pirate. Sly will be there to help but you need a few tips from a real pirate first.

SLY
Hey!

BONES
You're still in training, Sly. I'm about to be a full fledged pirate... especially if I... I mean her... she... whatever... when she brings back that jewel, we'll be the real deal.

FUCHSIA
This is so exciting.

(She claps and jumps happily)

SLY
She'll never pull it off. She's too girly.

BONES
Lesson 1... you can't be happy.

FUCHSIA
Never?

BONES
Never. Pirates are always grumpy and if something
good happens, they growl and get angry. It might
look like they are excited but they're not. They're
angry that it wasn't better. And they'll stay angry
until all the treasures of the world are theirs. And
then the anger dies down, they get grumpy again.

FUCHSIA
This will be hard... because I will be having so
much fun... but I will try.

BONES
Lesson 2... no baths, no washing, no cleaning up,
no perfume…

(Bones takes perfume from her and sprays herself happily. Bones sprays a little on
Sly and he coughs)

SLY
That's awful.

FUCHSIA
No perfume? Not even a little?

BONES
None. Pirate's take pride in their stench. It's like a
contest or something. And it makes it easier when
everyone smells bad. If you're the only one who
smells good, it's rough. It's better to blend in the
bad smells... it's like an orchestra of stink. If
someones out of tune, it throws off the balance.

SLY
Well said.

FUCHSIA
I shall adapt.

BONES
Lesson number... the next one...

SLY
Three, sir.

BONES
Whatever. You have to stop being so girly. Female pirates are the roughest, toughest, leanest, meanest human beings... nay... creatures! ...to ever travel the sea. If a male steals one gold doubloon, you steal two. If a male cuts off one finger, you cut off two.

FUCHSIA
Oh!

BONES
Too much for ye?

(Fuchsia smiles)

FUCHSIA
I'll adapt.

SLY
Me thinks she likes this a little too much.

BONES
Maybe she'll be okay.

FUCHSIA
More than okay... these will be the best days of my life so far!

BONES
So it's a deal then?

FUCHSIA
Wait... you're not ready to be a princess. My adventure depends on how successful you are in fooling everyone here.

BONES
Nothing to it. I just sit around, taking baths, putting
on perfume and eating chocolates.

(Bones finds some chocolate and eats it)

BONES (CONT.)
Oh, that's good.

(Sly tries to take some and Bones slaps his hand)

BONES (CONT.)
My chocolate.

FUCHSIA
I don't stay in the tower all the time. One of your
duties is to greet and entertain guests at the
upcoming royal ball.

BONES
Oh dear. You think I can fool everyone?

FUCHSIA
Ask that it be a costume party. That's not a strange
thing for me to request. I love to dress up. And be
sure to select a costume with a mask.

(Fuchsia runs in her room and then returns quickly with a funny
mask. She puts it on Bones. Sly laughs)

BONES
Seems simple enough.

FUCHSIA
You must also make your grand entrance. Let's
see your walk.

(Bones slouches and takes heavy steps. Sly chuckles)

FUCHSIA (CONT.)
You need a lot of work.

BONES
It's hard walking on a ship in the middle of the
ocean. I have a certain technique to keep me
steady.

FUCHSIA
A princess must float and glide through the air like
this.

(Fuchsia does a pretty walk. Sly nods in approval)

SLY
Nice.

FUCHSIA
Thank you.

(Bones tries to glide and float but looks very silly)

FUCHSIA
A little better.

SLY
Really?

FUCHSIA
Then you must greet each guest.

(Fuchsia holds her hand to Sly and does a curtsy. Sly shakes it hard)

SLY
Nice to meet ya!

FUCHSIA
No, no, no. You give me a kiss on my hand.

(Sly gets shy but gives her a kiss on the hand. Their eyes meet a moment and they smile
and then look away. Bones gives Sly a dirty look. She turns to Bones)

FUCHSIA
Now you try.

BONES
Fine.

(Bones does a silly floating walk up to Sly. She holds out her hand and does an odd curtsy.
Sly is nervous about kissing her hand.)

BONES (CONT.)
Go ahead... I won't hit you.

(Sly kisses her hand and then makes a weird face and spits)

SLY
What is on your hand? Yuck.

(Bones laughs)

FUCHSIA
You need some help... I know! My whipping boy!

BONES
Whipping boy?

FUCHSIA
Whenever I was bad, they'd spank my whipping
boy instead of me.

SLY
And I thought pirates were ruthless. That's terrible.

FUCHSIA
Don't criticize what you don't understand.

BONES
So how is this whipping boy going to help?

FUCHSIA
He and I are good friends actually.

BONES
Why in the world do you have a whipping boy?
And why would he be your friend?

FUCHSIA

Every princess needs a whipping boy. He was a
present for my 3rd birthday I think. My twos were
pretty terrible and they needed some way to punish
me... Or maybe to take out their frustrations... They
picked a nice servant boy I liked... We used to play
together... They thought if I saw him getting
whipped for something I did I would feel bad. They
were right. I felt terrible. It's horrible watching
someone you like getting hurt for something you did
wrong.

I always tried to make it up to him if he got whipped
in my place. I never liked to see him hurt so I tried
to be good... most of the time. When I messed up
and he got punished, then I'd try to do nice things
for him, like save him some of my favorite foods or
give him a little present. He ended up looking
forward to me getting in trouble because I was so
nice after. He's even tricked me in to being naughty
so he'd get punished and then rewarded. I wasn't
quite as nice that time. I don't like being tricked.

BONES
He sounds like pirate material to me.

FUCHSIA
Nope, he says he gets seasick. It's hard for him to
even come out here on the balcony and watch the
ocean, it makes him so sick.

SLY
Not pirate material.

BONES
So how does one end up becoming a whipping
boy?

FUCHSIA
His parents probably had some terrible debts and
they gave him up as payment.

SLY
What an awful way to settle a debt. Owe too much
money? Give us your first born child!

FUCHSIA
He said his family was very poor and that living in
the castle was a dream come true.

BONES
Even if it means he gets whipped and beat up.

SLY
He must have had it pretty bad.

FUCHSIA
I take good care of him. He'll be happy to help you.
He owes me.

BONES
If you say so...

FUCHSIA
You two hide... I'll see if I can find him.

(Sly and Bones go off to the rocks and Fuchsia disappears inside)

SLY
Have you gone mad?

BONES
It's win, win... win. Stinky gets the pink jewel, I get
a little bit of luxury and Fuchsia gets an adventure.

SLY
What about me? What do I get out of the deal?

BONES
Maybe you'll get the princess.

SLY
What?!

BONES
I saw the way you two looked at each other. She
thinks you're cute.

SLY
Really? Wait... no. I doubt it.

BONES
Handsome pirate like you... how can she resist?

SLY
Handsome? You resist all the time.

BONES
You're not my type.

SLY
What is your type?

(The whipping boy, Spud, enters with Fuchsia)

BONES
I don't know yet.

FUCHSIA
I need a big favor, Spud.

SPUD
Anything for you, Princess.

FUCHSIA
It's a secret though. You must swear not to tell
anyone. Not even Nanny. In fact you'll have to trick
her most of all.

SPUD
I am loyal to you most of all. I will do anything you
ask.

FUCHSIA
Anything?

SPUD
I give you my word and my life.

FUCHSIA
You are a good boy, Spud.

SPUD
You praise me too much. You honor me with your
trust in what sounds like a very important task.

FUCHSIA
Okay, you two can come out now.

(Sly and Bones appear. Spud jumps back but stands between them and the princess, ready
to defend her)

SPUD
Pirates!

FUCHSIA
It's okay. They're friends.

SPUD
How did you make such... friends?

FUCHSIA
Well... they made me a deal that I can't refuse.

SPUD
Dealing with pirates is like dealing with the devil.

BONES
I thought you said he'd be okay with this?

FUCHSIA
You will be... won't you, Spud?

SPUD
If it's what you wish, then it is what I will do.

FUCHSIA
It is my greatest wish... adventure.

SPUD
That is your greatest wish... you've told me of this
dream many times. And these two will grant it?

FUCHSIA
They will.

SPUD
How?

FUCHSIA
I will trade places with this girl.

BONES
Hi... I'm Bones.

(She starts to go toward him pirate wise for a shake of the hands, but switches to her odd
princess glide and tries to bow and holds out her hand. Spud reluctantly takes her hand and
is about it kiss it)

SLY
I wouldn't do that if I were you?

SPUD
Why? Is she yours?

(Bones pulls away her hand)

BONES
I belong to no one.

FUCHSIA
You will help Bones become me.

SPUD
What? That's impossible.

FUCHSIA
I know it won't be easy but if we're clever about it,
she can do it. We are about the same age and the
same height... same hair color.

SPUD
I suppose if she plays dress up a lot, like you do
sometimes.

FUCHSIA
That's a wonderful idea.

(To Bones)

FUCHSIA (CONT.)
I sometimes play dress up and wear costumes and
masks and talk in silly voices. It drives Nanny mad.
She totally avoids me when I act like that.

BONES
Perfect. Well done, Spud.

SPUD
I am pleased to serve.

FUCHSIA
Pretend like you're Lady Cuckoo and "talk like this."

(Fuchsia talks funny at the last part. Bones tries)

BONES
"'ello... I'm Lady Cuckoo and I talk like this."

FUCHSIA
Wonderful. This will work. Well done, Spud. Now
we need to get each other dressed.

BONES
"Lady Cuckoo is ready!"

(Bones and Fuchsia exit inside. Spud looks Sly over)

SPUD
So who are you?

SLY
Sly's me name. Pirating's me game.

                    SPUD
        That all it is to you... a game?

                    SLY
                  Sometimes.

                    SPUD
          Even when people get hurt?

                    SLY
              It's all part of the fun.

                    SPUD
    Horrible. I can't believe the princess wants to go
                    with you.

                    SLY
            I'll take good care of her.

                    SPUD
                  You better.

                    SLY
                That a threat?

                    SPUD
                     It is.

                    SLY
                   Oh yeah.

(Sly pulls out a knife or sword. Spud is lightning fast and grabs Sly's hand and squeezes
hard. Sly drops this weapon)

                 SLY (CONT.)
                  Hey! Stop it.

                    SPUD
                Useless pirate.

        (Spud lets go)

SLY
What's the big idea?

SPUD
I'm sorry... I'm just worried about the princess. This
is too dangerous.

SLY
I can keep her safe.

SPUD
If something happens to her... then something will
happen to Bones. You get my drift?

SLY
Uh... yeah.

SPUD
Bring her back to me, please.

SLY
You like her, don't you? A lot.

SPUD
More than life itself.

SLY
Have you told her that?

SPUD
Every day. She thinks it's silly... funny even. I know
she could never love a servant, but I can't help but
love her.

SLY
That's rough.

SPUD
So you can see how important it is to me that she
stay safe.

SLY
I do. I promise, first sign of danger, I'll get her off
the ship and back here. In fact, once she delivers
the jewel, there's no reason I can't turn around and
bring her right back.

SPUD
Jewel? What jewel?

SLY
Some big pink thing.

SPUD
Why are you taking that? It's worth a fortune.

SLY
That's what our captain wants and what Fuchsia
offered to us in exchange for changing places with
Bones.

SPUD
I have a bad feeling about this.

(Bones and Fuchsia return in different clothes. Fuchsia has Bones' pirate clothes plus a
patch over her eye and Bones is in a silly princess outfit)

SLY
Not bad.

FUCHSIA
Do I look piratey enough?

SLY
Yo ho ho.

FUCHSIA
I will take that as a yes.

BONES
How do I look?

SPUD
Never has there been a princess such as you to
walk this Earth.

BONES
Works for me.

SLY
Got the pink jewel?

FUCHSIA
Got it.

(She opens her bag. Sly is in awe)

SLY
Will you look at that?

BONES
Very impressive.

SPUD
And very expensive.

FUCHSIA
Everything daddy gives me is expensive. This won't
be missed.

SPUD
Let's hope not.

FUCHSIA
Ready for some adventure?!

SLY
Ay!

FUCHSIA
Then we be off. Take good care of Bones, Spud.

SPUD
I will, Princess.

(Spud pulls aside Sly)

SPUD
And you take good care of the Princess.

SLY
Pirate's honor.

SPUD
There's no such thing.

SLY
For her sake, you better hope their is.

FUCHSIA
I've never been rock climbing before. This will be
fun.

(She's gone)

SLY
Wait for me!

(Sly follows. Spud watches them go worried. Bones goes up to him)

BONES
I know Sly doesn't seem like much but he's a good
guy. Not very piratey at all.

SPUD
I hope not.

BONES
He's very loyal too. He's a good friend. You can
count on him.

SPUD
I appreciate you saying that. I just wish I could
believe it.

BONES
You care a lot about the Princess don't you?

SPUD
More than you can imagine.

BONES
But you're her whipping boy. She messes up and
you get beaten. Why would that inspire loyalty?

SPUD
She is very good to me. She treats me as a friend,
not a servant. Life with her has been so much
better than what I had before.

BONES
I see what you mean. This place is amazing... the
chocolate... I can't stop eating it... I have never
tasted anything so sweet. And the perfume... I
never thought anything could smell so good. And I
really really want to take a bath. Will the water
really be warm?

SPUD
Servants are heating water as we speak.

BONES
Is it really almost bath time? I'm in Heaven.

SPUD
But the nanny gives you the bath. How will you
bathe and still fool her?

BONES
Hmm... leave that to me.

(Bones puts on her mask goes inside)

BONES (CONT.)
Lady Cuckoo wants her bath alone. I don't want to
hear a single moan. Shoo shoo all of you. Or I will
kick you until you're black and blue!

(Nanny comes out on balcony)

NANCY
Fine, I will wait out here but I will come right back in
there if I hear you drowning.

BONES (OFF)
Always frowning on my drowning!

NANNY
She is very odd at times.

SPUD
Tell me about it. And I have a feeling she will be
weirder than usual.

NANNY
What's that in the distance?

SPUD
I don't see anything.

NANNY
Is that a ship? I don't like the look of that one.

SPUD
What's wrong with it?

NANNY
I knew a man who sailed a ship like that once. A
pirate!

SPUD
You don't like pirates?

NANNY
They stole my love from me.

SPUD
What happened?

NANNY

They lured him with talk of adventure and riches.
Yes, we were poor but I was happy. I didn't want
anything more. We had enough. But I guess it was
only enough for me... I should have told him that. I
wish I had said that more. I think he wanted to get
rich so he could marry me. But I would have
married him no matter how poor he was.

SPUD

But he left anyway.

NANNY

Life wasn't interesting enough with I guess. Oh,
who'd want a boring old lady like me?

SPUD

I wonder if he got the adventure he was looking
for?

NANNY

I don't know and I don't care. I hope his ship sank.

SPUD

You don't mean that.

NANNY

Maybe I do. Those pirates are bad news. They
promise adventure but only bring hurt and sadness
to all who dare cross their paths. Doom on all those
who tangle with pirates. Doom.

(Nanny goes back inside)

BONES (OFF)
Lady Cuckoo wants to be alone!

NANNY (OFF)
Keep your bubbles. I ain't looking.

BONES (OFF)
Away with you!

NANNY
I'm leaving.

SPUD
Doom? Oh, Fuchsia, what have I done?

BONES (OFF)
Lady Cuckoo was so cuckoo because she ate a
cuckoo pie.

END OF SCENE

SCENE 3

(Sly and Fuchsia arrive back on the pirate ship and are greeted by Stinky)

SLY
We have returned!

FUCHSIA
Argh!

STINKY
What? Already?

SLY
And we have the jewel!

FUCHSIA
Ay! Ay!

(FUCHSIA gives jewel to STINKY)

STINKY
I can't believe it. That's amazing, Bones.

(STICKY gives BONES a big slap on the back and FUCHSIA stumbles. SLY grabs her)

SLY
So is she a full pirate now?

FUCHSIA
Yo ho ho!

STINKY
Almost. She has one final test.

SLY
She does? What kind of test?

STINKY
You must face a final challenge, Bones. One that
will push you to your limits and prove to us all your
are worthy of the name pirate.

SLY

This is so unfair. She did the jewel thing. That was
pretty tough.

STINKY

Unfair? Ha! Since when are pirates fair? Quit your
whining, Sly. That's why you're only a polliwog.
Pirates don't whine. Right Bones?

FUCHSIA

Argh!

(STINKY slaps her on the back again and SLY catches her – he walks away)

SLY

Stop with all the goofy pirate talk.

FUCHSIA

Sorry… why are you so cranky?

SLY

Because we're in big trouble.

FUCHSIA

Why?

SLY

A final pirate test! To push you to your limits!
You're a princess not a pirate. How are you going
to survive an extreme test of your skills?

FUCHSIA

By being super cute?

SLY

Cute doesn't cut it here.

FUCHSIA

I have a great pout too.

(She shows him)

SLY
Nice… but that won't work either.

FUCHSIA
What if I cry?

(works on some tears)

SLY
Pirates don't cry. Stop that. Ever used a sword?

FUCHSIA
Never.

SLY
Ever used any kind of weapon?

FUCHSIA
Only in an emergency. But I prefer not to. I'm a
lady.

SLY
Not anymore. You're a pirate now… a very dead
pirate.

FUCHSIA
Dead? You're kidding right?

SLY
I hope so.

(STINKY looks at the jewel sadly)

FUCHSIA
Why is he so sad? Shouldn't he be happy?

SLY
I don't know. Let's spy on him and find out.

FUCHSIA
How rude.

SLY
But piratey – come on.

(FUCHSIA and SLY spy on him)

STINKY
Not enough time to work my plan… all I have is this silly jewel to show. What's wrong with me? Isn't it treasure I seek? No, it's love… the one thing a pirate can't have. I thought it was adventure I wanted. I left behind the one true love with promises I never could keep. Now she is some servant locked away in a castle. Nanny to some bratty princess. I wanted to rescue her and take her away from all that. I'd give up all the treasure in the world to have her again.

(STINKY leaves)

FUCHSIA
Oh my goonie gracious!

SLY
Such language. Watch your mouth.

FUCHSIA
Quiet you… I know who he is talking about. He's talking about my nanny!

SLY
So you're the bratty princess? That's funny.

FUCHSIA
You're impossible.

SLY
I try.

FUCHSIA
This means he is the long lost love that my nanny is always crying about. She still loves him. And he still loves her. This is so romantic.

SLY

Yuck… enough with the R word.

FUCHSIA

I totally have to play matchmaker… I have to bring
these two love birds back together again. That will
be my mission.

SLY

I thought you wanted to be a pirate? Pirates don't
play matchmaker.

FUCHSIA

Oh forget that. This is more important.

SLY

What about adventure? What about living life on
the edge? What about having some fun?

FUCHSIA

There's nothing more important than love. Show
me the way to my quarters. I must formulate a
plan.

(FUCHSIA exits)

SLY

She's going to love her "quarters"… I wonder what
she thinks of rats?

FUCHSIA

I'm waiting.

SLY

(sighs)

I really miss Bones.

END OF SCENE

SCENE 4

BONES
Time for my nap.

SPUD
But you slept in. How can you sleep again?

BONES
I'm making up for lost time. How much sleep do
you think I get on a pirate ship?

SPUD
But you have royal duties.

BONES
Royal what?

SPUD
Duties.

BONES
I made you say doodies.

SPUD
You're so weird.

BONES
But I'm the princess... I don't really have to do
anything important, do I?

SPUD
Of course you do. What if something were to
happen to the King? You're next in line to the
throne.

BONES
What?

SPUD
Well, Fuchsia is, and that's why she has her royal
duties. It prepares her for ruling the kingdom one
day.

BONES
But I can't do royal stuff... unless it's a royal flush in
poker or being a royal pain.

SPUD
You're really good at being a royal pain.

BONES
I just want baths and sleeps and eats. I don't want
any chores. I'm sick of chores.

SPUD
Duties.

BONES
Same thing.

SPUD
Shall I read your list of duties for today?

BONES
You can read?

SPUD
You can't?

BONES
I'm not saying.

SPUD
That could be a problem. I suppose that means you
can't write either. So much for letter writing today.

BONES
Letter writing?

SPUD
Thank you notes and such.

BONES
Thank you notes? Who writes thank you notes?

SPUD
Princesses.

BONES
Yuck.

SPUD
Then you have tea with Ambassador Melrose, his
wife and children.

BONES
Tea? Will there be sweets?

SPUD
Maybe but you can't eat them like you've been
eating everything else here. You have to be
proper.

BONES
Proper and pompous… boring.

SPUD
Then you have your music lessons.

BONES
What kind of music lessons?

SPUD
Singing. Can you sing?

(BONES sings a pirate song)

SPUD
Lovely.

BONES
Thanks… I'm well known at sea for my crooning.

SPUD
Oh, here's a fun one. You have to entertain your
little cousin, Princess Petunia.

BONES
Oh, great.

SPUD
Yeah, she's one of a kind.

BONES
I don't like your tone of voice. What's wrong with
her?

SPUD
You'll see.

BONES
Some help you are.

SPUD
Maybe if you weren't so difficult, I would be more
helpful.

BONES
What if I refuse to do them?

SPUD
Then I get whipped.

BONES
Fine.

SPUD
What?

BONES
Go get whipped. I'm not doing any of it.

SPUD
Don't you care at all what happens to me?

BONES
I've been whipped, stabbed, jabbed and punched
more times than I can count. And getting whipped
is your job. So go get whipped.

SPUD

Fine… you know what? I'll tell them you're ill or
something.

BONES

Good boy.

SPUD

Wow, pirates are terrible as I thought they'd be.
You're a piece of work.

BONES

Thank you… now scoot before I give you a good
whoopin' myself.

(SPUD bows)

SPUD

Your lowness.

(SPUD exits. BONES sighs when she is alone…)

BONES

I miss Sly… I wonder how Fuchsia is doing?

END OF SCENE

SCENE 5

(FUCHSIA follows SLY)

FUCHSIA

This is so exciting. I've always wanted to do
something really wonderful for nanny. She has
been so good to me over the years and I know if I
can pull this off and bring her the one true love of
her life, I'll make her happier than she's ever been.

SLY

Do you ever stop talking?

FUCHSIA

Every good princess must be able to converse with
ease.

SLY

Now I know why princesses and pirates don't get
along.

FUCHSIA

Oh, what's the matter grumpy guppy?

SLY

My rank is polliwog not guppy.

FUCHSIA

What's the matter my pouty polliwog?

SLY

Stop with the cuteness!

FUCHSIA

So are they going to have some kind of party for
me since I'm being made a full pirate?

SLY

Yes, the party is after the test... if you pass.

FUCHSIA

I'm a good student. I pass all my tests.

SLY
Prepare to get your first failing grade.

(STINKY enters)

STINKY
Bones… prepare yeself… your final challenge is
about to begin.

FUCHSIA
Yo ho ho!

SLY
She's doomed.

(A really big female pirate who looks mean and scary enters named Big
BERTHA)

BERTHA
Where be Bones?

(FUSHCIA is scared. SLY pushes her forward)

SLY
Here she be.

BERTHA
So ye thinks ye be a pirate eh?

(FUSHCIA is frozen with fear)

BERTHA
Speak or be splattered!

FUCHSIA
Splattered?

BERTHA
Crushed and splattered.

FUCHSIA
Sounds messy.

SLY

It is. I've seen her do it. You have to stand up to
her. That's part of the challenge.

FUCHSIA

How do I do that?

SLY

Talk back... don't Princesses ever talk back.

FUCHSIA

When we're really cranky.

SLY

Get cranky... or get dead.

FUCHSIA

I'll try.

BERTHA

You not be a pirate. You just be a little girl.

FUCHSIA

Takes one to know one.

(SLY rolls his eyes)

SLY

Nice one.

FUCHSIA

Thanks.

BERTHA

How can this be the great Bones? You are about as
scary as baby dolphin.

FUCHSIA

And you're... as ugly as an octopus.

BERTHA

Ha! You even insult like a little girl.

FUCHSIA

You know what you need? A makeover. You actually have nice eyes and with a good facial, you could really glow… and turn a few pirate eyes if you know what I mean.

BERTHA

What blasted nonsense are you talkin about?

FUCHSIA

It must be tough being a pirate gal these days. And very lonely.

BERTHA

I don't care for nothing… I don't need nothing…

FUCHSIA

We all need something… and you need some attention don't you? You're hair… those nails… those teeth… you're just crying for help.

BERTHA

No one helps me but myself.

FUCHSIA

There's nothing wrong with asking for a little help sometimes. Give me an hour… maybe two… maybe a day… and I could transform you into the most dazzling pirate woman in the seven seas. You want to get noticed? You want to turn heads? You want respect?

BERTHA

Ay… it be hard for a pirate woman to get respect round here.

FUCHSIA

So stop trying to look like them… stop trying to be like them… be yourself and be greater than them… you are woman… let them hear you roar.

BERTHA
Roar!

FUCHSIA
That was a figure of speech but an actual roar
works too. So what do you say? You want to
dazzle? You want respect? You want to beat these
men at their game or leave them speechless?

BERTHA
Ay!

FUCHSIA
Then come with me. We have some work to do
girl.

(FUCHSIA exits with BERTHA. STINKY goes up to SLY)

STICKY
What just happened?

SLY
I don't know.

END OF SCENE

SCENE 6

(BONES on castle balcony)

BONES
To be a pirate or a princess? I think I have a little
of both inside of me. I love to relax and be
pampered. I love chocolate and silky gowns and a
soft bed with satin sheets. But there's the other
side of me, the pirate side of me, that loves
adventure. I love the thrill of something new each
day... Good or bad... It's new and exciting and
makes me feel alive. And I miss the friendships I
have because a pirate is never alone. How could I
give up on my comrades, the ones who fight by my
side and tell me wonderful stories. I miss the tall
tales and the laughter. Instead I am locked away in
a tower... I suppose I have everything I need...
everything except a friend.

(Princess Petunia has heard some of this)

PETUNIA
Hello Fuchsia... I'm here.

BONES
Who are you?

PETUNIA
Princess Petunia... your favorite little cousin.

BONES
I'm ill... I don't wish to be observed...

PETUNIA
Observed... don't you mean disturbed?

BONES
Whatever.

PETUNIA
What's going on? You're not Fuchsia. I heard you
talking.

BONES
Quiet you… or you'll be in big trouble.

PETUNIA
Ha! You can't do anything to me. I'm a princess.

BONES
Well, I'm not so I can do plenty to you.

(Grabs her and holds to edge of balcony)

BONES
How about I throw you off the cliff here and into the
sea?

(PETUNIA squirms and bites BONES)

PETUNIA
I'm telling.

(BONES blocks her way)

BONES
You bit me! You sure you're a princess?

PETUNIA
I'm the meanest princess in the land. Just try to
stop me if you can.

BONES
Geez… do you have to speak in rhyme? That's
weird.

PETUNIA
Get out of the way. I will reveal your plot today.

BONES
Soon you will be a stiff; cause I'm throwing you off
the cliff.

(BONES grabs PETUNIA and gets ready to throw her off the balcony.
PETUNIA screams. NANNY rushes in. SPUD follows laughing)

NANNY
Stop this at once. What are you doing in here
Petunia?   Fuchsia is not feeling well today.

PETUNIA
Spud said I could come in.

BONES
Of course he did.

(SPUD smiles evily at BONES)

NANNY
You are an impossible little girl, Petunia. Where is
your nanny?

(Fake innocence)

PETUNIA
I don't know.

NANNY
What did you do to her this time? That poor lady.

SPUD
She sent her on some wild goose chase looking for
some sweet cream for her supper.

NANNY
The last thing you need is sweet cream.

PETUNIA
Are you saying I'm fat? You horrid woman. I'm
telling my daddy!

NANNY
You will do no such thing.

PETUNIA
I will tell him you hit me… then you'll be in big
trouble.

BONES
How about I throw you off the cliff instead?

(BONES grabs PETUNIA)

NANNY
As much as I'd enjoy seeing that… we better not.
Come with me Petunia… we shall have a little
lesson in manners…

PETUNIA
What if I don't?

NANNY
Then I will hit you and I will enjoy it.

PETUNIA
Later pirate.

(NANNY leaves with PETUNIA)

SPUD
She knows?

BONES
She heard me talking to myself.

SPUD
This is bad… she'll tell everyone.

BONES
What do we do?

SPUD
I have no clue… this is your mess…

BONES
You're the one who let her in here… we wouldn't be
in this mess now if it weren't for you. Fuchsia
would be pretty upset if she knew you pulled a
prank like that.

SPUD

Poor Fuchsia. I hope she is okay.

BONES

Something is up over there too. My ship is still on
the horizon. They should have set sail by now.

SPUD

I can take a boat... and go check on her.

BONES

I'll go with you.

SPUD

They'll never let you out of the castle. Fuchsia is
never allowed to leave.

BONES

She's a prisoner?

SPUD

She's being protected.

BONES

I'll never go anywhere... see anything...

SPUD

You're stuck.

BONES

I'm going a little stir crazy... I'm not sure I can do
this.

SPUD

So you want to switch back?

BONES

Maybe.

SPUD

I'll go get Fuchsia.

BONES
Don't you get seasick?

SPUD
I will manage.

BONES
Good luck... she's either having the time of her life
or a prisoner by now... either way she's not coming
easily.

SPUD
It's worth it.

BONES
You like her don't you?

SPUD
Yes... she treats me well.

BONES
More than that... you have feelings for her... strong
feelings.

SPUD
That's none of your business.

BONES
But you're a lowly servant and she is a princess.
She can never love you yet you love her. How sad.

SPUD
That's enough. Keep your thoughts to yourself. Or
I'll throw you off the cliff.

BONES
I'd like to see you try.

SPUD
I'm going for Fuchsia... you think you can handle
yourself?

BONES
No problem.

SPUD
Good luck.

BONES
You too, Spud.

(SPUD exits. NANNY enters)

NANNY
What's going on here?

BONES
What do you mean?

NANNY
You're not Fuchsia.

BONES
Ooops… forgot my mask didn't I?

NANNY
Where is she? Where is Fuchsia?

BONES
Calm down… everything's okay. Spud went to go
get her.

NANNY
Where?

BONES
Out there… on the pirate ship.

NANNY
You are a pirate! Guards!

BONES
No… no… wait.

NANNY
I should have known pirates were behind this. You
are an evil lot. Guards!

BONES
Time to make my exit... off the cliff I go.

(BONES rips off her skirt and heads off the
balcony)

NANNY
Guards! Hurry! She is escaping!

END OF SCENE

SCENE 7

SLY
So you survived the challenge?

FUCHSIA
Yes.

SLY
By giving Big Bertha a makeover?

FUCHSIA
Yes.

SLY
I don't understand anything anymore.

STINKY
I understand.

SLY
You do?

STINKY
This isn't Bones is it?

SLY
Sure it is.

STINKY
Where is she? And who is this?

FUCHSIA
I'm Princess Fuchsia.

STINKY
From the castle? THE Princess Fuchsia… heir to
the throne?

FUCHSIA
The one and the same.

STINKY
I should throw you in the brig. You'd make a
mighty fine hostage. We could ransom you for a
King's fortune.

SLY
I captured her…

FUCHSIA
What?

SLY
Play along… I'll get you out of this.

(SLY turns to STINKY)

SLY (CONT.)
I captured her and I get to say what's what with my
prison. That be the pirate law.

STINKY
Ay… but you're not a pirate yet are ye?

SLY
I'm close.

STINKY
Not close enough. So I'll be taking her as my
prisoner… to the brig.

(SPUD rushes on board. He is very seasick but trying to appear ready.
He has a sword)

SPUD
Unhand her, scoundrel!

STINKY
Who are you?

SPUD
I'm Spud and I'm here to rescue Fuchsia.

FUCHSIA
Really?

STINKY
You a prince or something?

FUCHSIA
He is in my book.

SPUD
Alas, I am but a humble servant... but I have sworn
to protect her with my life.

STINKY
Kill him, Sly.

SLY
What?

STINKY
You want to be a pirate? Then kill him.

SLY
Uh... okay.

(SLY goes after SPUD with a sword)

FUCHSIA
No!

SLY
Sorry, Fuchsia. I know we have become friends.
And I know you care for Spud, but I am a pirate first
and I must defend my ship. And I never avoid a
good fight, even if my opponent is outmatched by
my skill as a swordsman...

(SPUD quickly knocks the sword out of his hand and knocks him down
and pins him with his foot and points the sword at him)

STINKY
Get him Bertha!

(BERTHA enters and is done up all pretty)

BERTHA
I don't feel like fighting anymore. I might break a
nail.

STINKY
This is madness!

(STINKY goes after SPUD. They have a dramatic sword fight. STINKY
overpowers SPUD and knocks his sword away)

FUCHSIA
No!

(SLY holds her back)

STINKY
Any last words?

(NANNY enters with BONES)

NANNY
Please wait!

(STINKY stops and is shocked)

STINKY
Janice?

NANNY
Yes… it's me, Eugene.

(STINKY takes her hands and they walk off stage or upstage during the following)

SLY
Eugene? That's Stinky's real name?

STINKY
What are you doing here?

NANNY
A very unusual girl brought me here.

BONES
That's me... Bones the Unusual.

SLY
What are you doing here?

BONES
I got bored of being pampered.   But I had a bath
and I should be good for another month or two.

SLY
It's good to have you back... I missed you...

BONES
Well, I didn't miss you... much.

SPUD
How did you get out of the castle?

BONES
Well, the Nanny there found me out thanks to that
little brat Petunia. So I jumped off the balcony and
climbed down the cliff. But then the guards had me
surrounded at the bottom. So I convinced the
Nanny to loan me a boat so we could rescue
Fuchsia.

SPUD
I was rescuing Fuchsia.

BONES
I figured you'd need some help.

SLY
You were right.

FUCHSIA
Don't listen to them Spud. I thought you were very
brave.

SPUD
But I failed you, princess.

FUCHSIA
But you came and risked your life… that means so
much to me.

SPUD
You humble me with your kind words.

BONES
So what's the deal with Stinky and the nanny.

FUCHSIA
They are long lost loves. You've brought them
together again.

BONES
Is that the woman Stinky is always blubbering
about.

FUCHSIA
It is.

BONES
Well, what do you know?

FUCHSIA
Looks like you're a matchmaker.

BONES
A matchwhater?

FUCHSIA
A matchmaker. You brought two lonely hearts
together.

BONES
Ew. I did that. Gross.

FUCHSIA
Maybe you brought more lonely hearts together
than that.

(FUCHSIA takes SPUD by the hand)

SPUD
But princess…

FUCHSIA
Row me home, Spud?

SPUD
Of course.

FUCHSIA
Slowly.

SPUD
I brought your parasol and a picnic.

FUCHSIA
You're amazing as usual.

(BONES and SLY watch them go. NANNY and STINKY come forward)

NANNY
Come home with me… I miss you.

STINKY
I be missing you too.

NANNY
I would do anything to have you home again.

STINKY
Even rub my feet?

NANNY
Even rub your feet.

STINKY
You give the best foot rubs. Let's go home. You
have the bridge, Bertha.

BERTHA
Ay! Ay!

(NANNY and STINKY leave)

SLY
Wow, I feel sorry for any woman who has to rub
those feet.

BONES
That's true love.

SLY
True love indeed.

(SLY looks at BONES)

BONES
The only I love I have is the sea.

SLY
Yeah... me too.

BERTHA
Set sail for Paris! I want to do some shopping.

(BERTHA exits)

BONES
It's good to be home.

END OF PLAY

Made in United States
North Haven, CT
27 March 2023

34601494R00039